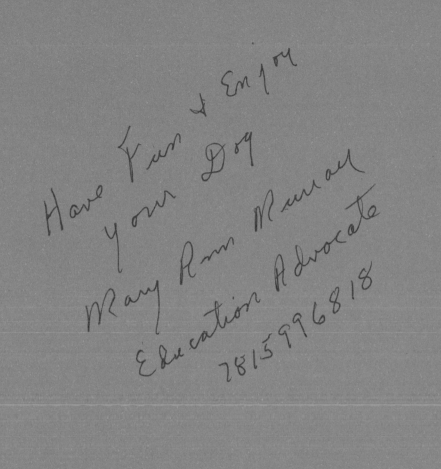

Have Fun & Enjoy
Your Dog

Mary Ann Murnau

Education Advocate

7815996818

Dog Tricks

Dog Tricks

40 fun activities for you and your dog!

Selina Gibsone
and Jenny Palser

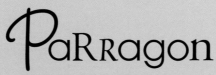

PaRragon

Bath New York Singapore Hong Kong Cologne Delhi Melbourne

First published by Parragon in 2009
Parragon
Queen Street House
4 Queen Street
Bath BA1 1HE, UK

ISBN: 978-1-4075-5557-7
Printed in China

Created and produced by Ivy Contract
Editorial Director: Tom Kitch
Art Director: Lisa McCormick
Senior Editor: Polita Caaveiro
Designers: Glyn Bridgewater and Kate Haynes
Photographer: Nick Ridley
Model: Cynthia McCollum

Ivy Contract would like to thank Millie Smith and all the
trainers at the Hearing Dogs for Deaf People organization
for all their help with producing this book.

CONTENTS

INTRODUCTION

This book is all about having fun and enjoying spending time with your dog—and perhaps showing off how clever he is! The step-by-step training it provides will not only strengthen that all-important doggie–human bond, but will teach your dog new skills and boost his confidence. One of the reasons why dogs make such good pets is the wonderful way they communicate with people. Training will not only help you to understand how your dog communicates, it will also help your dog to interpret your cues correctly. By following the positive methods used in this book, both you and your dog can enjoy these tricks—and the applause—for many years to come.

Why train tricks?

If you have a dog already, or are planning to get one soon, it is important to think about the time you have available. Dogs require much more than just food and water. They need plenty of fresh air, exercise, and stimulation, as well as praise and interaction. By taking the time to teach your dog these clever tricks, you can help to keep your dog physically and mentally fit as well as contented. And that's not to mention the equivalent benefits that can come your way—it's a great way to stay in shape, and who would say no to a set of paws that can close doors and give you a high five?

The tricks in this book range from basic obedience to more advanced exercises that focus on agility, so if you have not done any training before, this book will cover all you need to know. There are 40 tricks to work through, with more than enough for all the family to enjoy, from the basic "sit" and "stay" to the impressive "acting shy" and "jump through hoops" tricks. Whatever the level of the trick you decide to tackle, try to keep your sessions short so your dog does not become too tired or full up with treats. Also, it is always important to end your training on a good note. If it becomes too difficult, or you try to rush the steps, you may find that your dog stops having fun. And that probably means you've stopped having fun, too! In this book, your dog is referred to as "him"—however, male and female dogs can be equally successful at learning any trick, as shown by our dog models.

How does your dog learn?

Dogs learn by understanding that their behavior has a consequence. If the consequence is good, they are more likely to repeat the behavior. For example, if your dog sits, he learns that he gets a treat and some praise; he'll probably try his luck and sit again. If your dog jumps up, he may learn that you ignore him and turn away. If your dog learns that he receives no attention when he jumps up, he is less likely to repeat the behavior and more likely to sit instead. This principle is the basis of dog training.

It is a good idea to make sure desirable behavior is followed by good things, so that when you give your dog treats and praise, you are always rewarding his behavior. Any wrong or undesirable behavior needs to be ignored in order to prevent your dog from associating your command voice with being told off. With this in mind, this book encourages the use of treats while training the tricks. By making sure that you select treats that are small and quick to eat, you can help keep your dog focused and prevent him from getting full during a training session. If your dog is prone to putting on weight, you may want to use portions of his dinner for training. Alternatively, you can use toys as the reward if your dog enjoys a game.

The majority of the tricks in this book are trained using the treat in your hand to lure your dog into the correct position before you offer the reward of the treat. As a result, your dog may initially be more focused on your hand because he will associate it with food. It is, therefore, important to complete the training by removing the treat from your hand. This way you can be sure that your dog really understands each trick. When your dog is confident, you can try to put together a sequence of moves, rewarding him occasionally throughout. By giving your dog rewards intermittently, you may find that the behavior becomes stronger and that your dog may try even harder to get the reward.

Top Tip A clicker can help in training, because it makes it easier for your dog to understand exactly what he is being rewarded for. However, as the click is so precise, you must be confident in your timing.

Training tools

In this book, you will see that desired behaviors are most often rewarded using your voice—"good boy" goes a long way!—some tasty tidbits, or even a toy. However, there are additional aids used by any good dog trainer that can put you on the path toward having a well-trained and clever dog.

Just a click away...

In dog training, you will find that many people use what is known as a "clicker" (shown above left). This small plastic box makes a sound that your dog can associate with the arrival of a treat, and lets your dog know the precise moment he is doing something right. For example, if you are training your dog to sit, as he moves into the correct position, click and reward him immediately with a treat.

By using a clicker, you can make training easier and quicker for your dog. If you would like to use a clicker as you work through the book, simply follow the steps explained, and use the clicker at the appropriate time before rewarding your dog with a treat. First, however, you will need to tune your dog into the sound. To do this, simply click and then produce a treat for your dog. Repeat this step until your dog is responding to the sound reliably and looking at you for his treat. Make sure at this stage you do not inadvertently click your dog when he is doing something wrong—you may find that he repeats this behavior a little more than you would have liked!

You can even use a "clicker word" in the same way. By associating a word, such as "good," with the arrival of a treat, you can say "good" as your dog does something well, and then give the reward.

Using voice and hands

You will notice in this book that your dog is always taught to perform the desired behavior before any commands are begun. In this way, you can ensure that your dog associates each command with the correct behavior. For example, it allows your dog to first learn how to sit, and then when to sit.

Most of the tricks in this book suggest a word as the command. However, if you prefer, you can use a hand signal. You will often see trainers using hand signals, particularly when they are working their dog at a distance. Some dogs may be more responsive to body language than others, so why not try both and see which your dog prefers.

How to be a good trainer

A good dog trainer needs patience, consistency, good timing, and most importantly a love of dogs—especially when it comes to the "kissing cousins" trick! It is important not to rush your dog's training, or expect too much too quickly. Be patient and calm and always begin training when you have plenty of time. Choose an area that is quiet with few distractions at first, especially when you are starting a new trick. Once your dog grows in confidence, you can build up distractions by practicing outside and even in a busy park.

In order for your dog to understand exactly what you want from him, you must be consistent. This is important not only during training sessions, but also in your everyday life together. Your dog doesn't understand if you are having a bad day and will still continue to learn from the way that you interact with him. Remember, it's better to reward your dog when he does something good, and to ignore him if he does something you don't like. Try to think carefully about what your dog may learn in any situation and remember to be consistent.

Keep your dog motivated

It is important that your dog is motivated when starting a training session. If your dog is not interested in the toy or treat that you are using, it's pretty likely that he won't complete each trick. Choose your reward carefully and work out what really motivates your dog for those tricks that require plenty of concentration. Some of these tricks are difficult, and your dog must believe it's worth the effort.

To keep your training sessions interesting, vary the treats and toys that you use. Also, be aware of mealtimes. If your dog has just eaten his dinner before a session, he may be full before you even get started! Try to hold back those special toys and treats for use during training. If your dog learns that he can get his favorite things at any time, he will be less likely to work in order to obtain them.

If your dog is finding something difficult, take a short break. Try again after a while and remember you may need to go back a stage to make it a little easier. If your dog starts to switch off, try using a more exciting reward that should help to keep your dog interested and focused.

Timing is everything...

Timing is one of the most important things to remember when training your dog. The reward should happen at the precise moment that your dog is doing something right. Rewarding too early could distract your dog from what he is doing—rewarding too late may confuse your dog and he may not understand what he is being praised for. After your dog completes each trick, remember to provide a treat and some praise, such as "good boy!"

How to use this book

This book has been written to help you teach your dog a number of clever tricks, but first you must learn the basics. To do this, start by working through the initial obedience commands in the first chapter of the book. As you and your dog grow in confidence you can try out the more advanced tricks—fancy hoops and poles, here we come!

Laying down the groundwork

These first chapters can be the most important; they not only lay down the foundation for the trick training, but also help with general manners and good all-round doggy behavior. Some of the exercises in this chapter will also help to show off your dog in the park by teaching him to return to you, sit, lie down, and stay. The more advanced tricks often involve some of these earlier exercises, so it's a good idea to work through the book in order.

Certain breeds may find some tricks easier than others, and this has been highlighted where appropriate. The "fetch" command, for example, can be harder for some dogs that might not naturally enjoy retrieving. This means that you may have to work harder to get results, or may need to try a different trick. If your dog does not want to try a specific trick, don't push it. Remember—any training that you do with your dog is about having fun!

If your dog is older, forget the popular saying—it isn't true that you can't teach him any new tricks. You may, however, find that some tricks are potentially unsuitable or that your dog finds certain positions uncomfortable. Be sensible and don't persist with the training if you think your dog is not happy—there are plenty of other tricks that may be more appropriate.

Agility training

The last chapter in this book focuses on agility. Dog agility is a great sport that can be a lot of fun for you and your dog, keeping you both in tip-top condition! Agility tricks can be taught just for enjoyment, or you can take them to another level and try agility competitions in the future. Think big!

Any size of dog can take part in agility, and the competitions are carefully divided by size and skill level—so don't worry, you won't be competing against the top dogs straight away! If you are thinking of competing, the best idea is to find a good agility class where you can use all the equipment safely. Don't be tempted to use equipment that is unsafe or homemade; this could be dangerous and may knock your dog's confidence if something goes wrong. Find yourself a qualified agility instructor and he or she will be able to advise you on how to register your dog for competitions and ensure that he is trained appropriately for all the agility obstacles.

Staying safe and sound

Safety is important for both you and your dog and you will find that some of the tricks in the book are more suitable for certain breeds. Due to their body shape, some breeds may find it more difficult to balance in various positions. The same will apply if you have an older dog. Although trick training can be less energetic than many exercises, be careful when choosing the different tricks because your dog may tire more easily. If your dog is pregnant or has any health problems that you are unsure about, always check with your veterinarian before you start training.

Safe surroundings

Make sure you always train in safe surroundings. Some tricks, such as the "doggy dance," may be more suitable on carpet or grass, because they involve trying to achieve a balancing position. Agility is best trained outside where there is plenty of room for your dog to run around. Most agility clubs train on grass or in a horse ménage and avoid any hard or slippery floors. It is important to remember that if the grass is wet, the equipment is possibly wet too, so take it steady and this will help to avoid any injuries.

The retrieving exercises in the book involve your dog picking up a variety of items. Make sure the items you choose are safe, and remember not to use anything with small parts that your dog could swallow or choke on. Put all items out of reach when you leave your dog alone—this way you will avoid any unwanted chewing when you are not around!

We hope that you and your dog enjoy working through this book together and remember—whatever happens, have fun!

Trick tips

- Plan your training session
- Always use treats and toys to motivate your dog
- Practice and perfect your timing
- Always have water available
- Stay patient
- Keep training sessions fun
- Always end on a good note
- Start training early in your dog's life
- Be consistent
- Have fun!

GROUNDWORK

SITTING PRETTY

by JD

The "sit" is one of the key obedience commands and can be taught from an early age. It can be helpful in many different situations, from preventing your puppy from jumping up for attention to keeping your dog under control when crossing roads. Keep sessions short—it's important that your dog enjoys the training, even if the trick takes a bit longer to learn. As with all the tricks, make sure you practice in plenty of different places. Your dog may soon know how to sit politely in the lounge, but this might not extend to the park!

"GOOD BOY!"

"SIT!"

1 Hold a treat in front of your dog's nose and, with an upward hand movement, raise the treat above your dog's head. Your dog should try to follow the treat by moving its head upward.

Top Tip Once you've mastered this trick, hold your hand out flat without a treat, then raise it toward your shoulder to lure your dog into the sit position. He will start to learn the hand signal for "sit," and you won't have to rely on treats!

2 As the head goes up, gravity should now move your dog's rear toward the floor. Be patient—especially if your dog is young—pushing his rear onto the floor may put your dog off in the future. Encourage your dog with praise.

3 With his rear on the floor, you can now give your dog the treat and some more praise. Once you have mastered this sit position, you can start adding the word "sit" just before your dog's rear touches the floor.

13

STAYING POWER

by FERN

For the "stay" command—an extension of "sit," really—the dog learns to remain in a still position until asked to move. The "stay" is an invaluable safety tool and can be used when your dog is getting out of a car, going indoors and outdoors, and when off his leash in the park. As before, make sure to train your dog to "stay" in plenty of different places. Build your training slowly and add enticing distractions, such as other dogs running around and people playing ball. With practice, you will have the best-trained dog in the park!

"SIT!"

1 Ask your dog to "sit" and with an extended hand take a small step away, keeping eye contact. This will begin to teach your dog the hand signal for the "stay" position.

Top Tip Slowly build up the distance from your dog and also the time delay between saying "stay" and returning to your dog. If you rush, your dog may ignore your command, undoing all your hard work.

"GOOD GIRL!"

2 Wait a few seconds, then holding your palm flat, say "stay" in a serious tone before stepping toward your dog. If your dog has remained in the sit position, provide a treat and plenty of praise, such as "good girl!" If your dog moves, don't worry—wait for a couple of seconds and try again, taking your dog back to the position where he was originally told to stay.

See also...

Sitting pretty, p. 13

3 When your dog is reliably staying in a position, continue to use the voice command "stay." Keep using the hand signal, which can be especially useful if your dog is at a distance from you.

"STAY!"

GET DOWN ON IT
by LEO

With training, your dog should quickly learn that paying attention can be rewarding. The more tricks you teach, the easier the learning process becomes and your dog should start to respond quicker to each new exercise. With the "sit" position complete, we are halfway to achieving the "down" position, which dogs can learn from a very young age. This position will help to settle your dog in different environments, such as at a store or at mealtimes, and it will help you stop your dog from jumping up at visitors as they come into the house.

"SIT!"

1 From the "sit" position, get your dog's attention by holding out a treat in front of you. Make sure you choose a really tasty treat, because you are going to ask your dog to follow this morsel to the floor.

2 Slowly move your hand with the treat down toward the floor. Your dog should follow it, lowering his body on the way to lying down. Don't worry if your dog doesn't lie down immediately—wait with the treat on the floor, and it should soon happen. Only release the treat once your dog is down, and remember to give your dog plenty of praise.

"GOOD BOY!"

See also...
Sitting pretty, p. 13
In your bed, p. 48

3 Repeat the steps until your dog is happily lying down every time. You can then start to add the command "down," remembering to reward your dog and give plenty of praise. When your dog is consistently lying down, gradually delay the release of the treat. Varying the time before treating in this way will help keep your dog focused.

"DOWN!"

COME ON OVER

by RIVA

The "come" command trains dogs to come back from wherever they have been roaming. It is important that you can call your dog back to you at any time, especially if there's any danger. Training early helps prevent problems as your dog grows up, and you will need to continue this work by praising and rewarding your dog for a successful return. Never shout, even if your dog doesn't come back straight away—he will think that coming back is the wrong thing to do! Practice in different places, building up slowly to increasingly exciting distractions.

1 In a quiet area, get your dog's attention and have some yummy treats ready. Show your dog a treat and gradually move away. Your dog should start to follow you (well, the treat, actually).

2 Use your dog's name and the word "come"—in this case, "Come, Riva!" Encourage your dog to come toward you by providing a treat and plenty of fuss on approach. This teaches your dog that coming toward you is fun, exciting, and potentially tasty.

"COME, RIVA!"

3 Repeat steps one and two until your dog is reliably coming back to you when you call. Try it without the treat in your hand. Your dog should "come" on command, allowing you to shower him with praise for being so clever! Gradually practice the recall in different places, teaching your dog to respond even when distracted.

"GOOD GIRL!"

Top Tip Tone of voice and body language is key to achieving this command—be firm and consistent.

See also...

Sitting pretty, p. 13

16

DROP IT, LEAVE IT
by WHISPER

You can start using this command from puppyhood to any age. Some dogs love to pick up everything, especially things they shouldn't have. By using the "drop it" command correctly, your dog will be happy to give up even your smelly socks in return for a tasty treat. This exercise uses toys, but sometimes your dog may pick up something far too exciting, such as a chicken bone—if this happens, you will need to use a nicer treat to encourage the "drop." Never chase your dog during this command, or it will become a (very tiring) game.

"GOOD BOY!"

1 Wait until your dog has the chosen toy in its mouth, then fish out a treat. At this stage, make it easy on yourself and only use a toy that your dog would be happy to give up!

2 Once your dog shows interest in the treat, the toy should naturally "drop." As this happens, pick up the toy and at the same time give your dog the treat and plenty of praise.

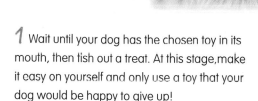

See also...
Go fetch!, p. 19
Fetch a specific item, p. 32

3 Once your dog starts to drop the toy reliably, add the command "drop it." You can then progress with this exercise by asking your dog to "drop it" without using the treat in your hand and simply pointing to the ground. Always reward your dog after a drop. Your dog will soon be happy to swap any item for something that you have.

"DROP IT!"

SIMPLE FAVORITES

GO FETCH!
by RIVA

A dog taught to "fetch" will retrieve any item on command. This can be a great game to strengthen your doggy–human relationship (and tire you out). It will encourage your dog to stay closer to you on a walk and be less likely to run off or be distracted by other dogs and animals. Make sure your "fetch" items are safe—for example, never throw sticks because they can injure your dog. Some breeds will enjoy playing fetch games more than others. Labradors and spaniels will naturally enjoy carrying items, but others may need encouragement.

"GOOD GIRL!"

"FETCH!"

Top Tip Dog not interested in toys? Try food! First, give your dog a treat for just a sniff of the toy. Next, wait for your dog to put its mouth around a toy before offering a treat. He'll soon pick up anything in return for a treat!

"DROP!"

2 Throw the toy and, using a lot of praise, encourage your dog to bring the toy back, making sure to offer a treat if this succeeds. When your dog is reliably retrieving the toy, add the command "fetch."

3 If your dog already knows the "drop" command, use this when your dog returns with the toy, and offer a treat and praise. If your dog really enjoys the fetch game, offer an additional reward by throwing the toy each time it's brought back successfully. You'll be shocked at just how long this game can go on!

1 Tease your dog playfully with a favorite toy by moving it around on the floor just out of reach. When your dog goes to pick up the toy, say "good boy!" and offer a treat.

Simple favorites

LET'S SHAKE ON IT

by WHISPER

"Shaking hands" teaches your dog to place his paw in your outstretched hand. Once your dog is confident shaking your hand, you can start to teach him to "shake hands" with family and friends. This is a great trick for when people visit, because they can all greet your dog with a "handshake" when they enter the house! You can even teach your dog different commands for each paw, such as using a right or left paw when asked. This trick can become part of your regular health-checking routine, making it easier to check your dog's feet and nails.

"SIT!"

"GOOD BOY!"

"SHAKE HANDS!"

1 Ask your dog to "sit" (see page 13), then hold a treat in a closed fist in front of your dog just below his nose. Your dog should start to show interest in the food and try to get it out of your hand.

See also...

Sitting pretty, p. 13
Bye-bye!, p. 38

2 Your dog may sniff and lick your hand at first, but will eventually try to use a paw to get the treat. If your dog raises a paw at all, offer loads of praise and encouragement with your voice.

3 When your dog touches your hand with a paw, open it, revealing the treat (which will be quickly eaten). Repeat the above steps until your dog is reliably lifting a paw to your hand. Now start adding the "shake hands" command. To complete the trick, put your hand out without the treat and ask to "shake hands."

HI THERE!

by BLITZ

Make those doggy vocal chords useful by employing a toy to teach your dog to bark or "say hi" on command. Be careful—if your dog barks a lot, you may not want to teach this trick (unless you have good earplugs). Likewise, if your dog does not bark at all, think carefully before encouraging this behavior. Never reward your dog for barking at people in or out of the house, because this can turn into a problem. To train this trick, you will need to find something your dog likes—if not a special toy, then nice treats can go a long way.

"GOOD BOY!"

Top Tip Use a "quiet" command when your dog stops barking. Here, you give the dog a treat after a quiet spell. This helps ensure your dog does not bark for long periods. Never reward your dog for a bark unless you have asked for this behavior.

1 Show your dog a favorite toy and keep it out of reach. Your dog may start to get excited and jump to get the toy. Make sure you hold tight and keep it out of reach!

2 Your dog should become more frustrated and may bark. At this point, give your dog loads of praise. It may take some time for the barking to begin, so be patient!

3 Reward your dog for barking by finally offering the toy and playing a game. Repeat the steps until your dog starts to bark as soon as you withhold the toy. Now you can add the command "say hi." It is important to match this trick with the command quickly, because you don't want the dog to learn to bark in other situations.

"SAY HI!"

TAKE A BOW

by CEDAR

You will hopefully have seen your dog naturally "bow" when playing with other dogs in the park. By training the "take a bow" trick you can teach your dog to show off this impressive position on command. It's a spectacular trick that can be incorporated at the end of a routine. Remember you can always use a visual cue for any of our tricks. For example, the visual cue for the bow could be you going into a bow position and your dog would respond by doing the same. This should really wow your friends (or at least get some applause)!

Safety This trick is not suitable for an elderly, arthritic dog or one with a bad back. Be careful if your dog has any injuries or joint problems. If you have any concerns, consult a veterinarian.

"GOOD GIRL!"

"BOW!"

1 While your dog is in a standing position, get his attention and then hold a treat in front of his nose. Slowly bring the treat down toward the floor between your dog's front paws.

2 As soon as your dog's front legs are flat on the floor, offer a treat and some praise. Your dog may try to put his back end down and lie down completely, so you will have to get your treat in quickly before this happens.

3 Once your dog is reliably going into the "take a bow" position, add the command "bow." You can also try to make your dog hold the position for longer before you provide a treat (encore, encore).

KISSING COUSINS

by PIPPA

Some dogs are really affectionate and enjoy showing their owners affection by giving them a big lick on the face! This "kiss" is a simple trick and will reward your dog for something he naturally enjoys. And let's face it, it's nice to be appreciated for all those walks. By matching this trick with a command, your dog should perform the behavior only when asked. Think about this before training, because friends may not be so welcoming of a wet dog kiss! Reward your dog for a gentle kiss and not anything that encourages him to become too rough.

1 Sit down on the floor with your dog and start to make a fuss of him. Don't hold a treat in your hand at this stage because your dog will be distracted. Instead, have some treats ready in your pocket.

"GOOD GIRL!"

3 Continue to make a fuss of your dog and he should start to lick your face. As soon as he does, give him loads of praise and a treat from your pocket. Your dog will start to work out what the treat is for and repeat the trick. Now add the command "kiss" when your dog licks your face, and praise him enthusiastically. Always give the command "down" when you want to finish.

2 Encourage your dog to give you more affection. If he is happy to, you can ask your dog to jump up and put his front feet on your shoulders. If your dog is smaller, you can do this with him sitting on your lap.

"KISS!"

JUMP FOR JOY
by PIPPA

What a fun trick for your dog to enjoy—something akin to being paid to jump on the bed! You'll need plenty of room to train because your dog may become excited. This is an exuberant trick and not suitable for young puppies, older dogs, those with joint problems, or a giant breed, because it puts pressure on their joints. Many dogs pick up this trick quickly, but it may take a few weeks for your dog to perform it on command. Train in a safe environment, free of clutter, and avoid anywhere that your dog may struggle to get his footing.

1 Get your dog's attention and hold a treat up high, out of reach. Use a treat your dog really wants, because he will have to put some effort into getting it! If your dog prefers toys, you can hold one of these instead.

2 As your dog tries to reach the treat, he may start to lift his front legs off the floor. At this point, praise your dog, but then raise the treat even higher, so he can't reach it even when standing up on his hind legs.

"JUMP UP!"

"GOOD GIRL!"

3 Encourage your dog to jump up for the treat, giving lots of praise and a treat as soon as a little jump occurs. Give your dog a rest and try again, this time giving a reward for jumping that little bit higher. When the trick is mastered, add the command "jump up."

Top Tip If you would rather not use a verbal command, an effective hand signal is to simply raise your hand up high.

See also...

Doggy dance, p. 41
Jump on a chair, p. 46

24

ROLL OVER

by PECAN

The "roll over" is a fun and easy trick to teach your dog. First, make sure that your dog has learned the "down" position. Your dog may learn this trick quickly, because many dogs like to roll around naturally, often not in the nicest places! If your dog is less inclined to be prone, give plenty of encouragement and work through the steps slowly. First, let your dog become confident lying on his side; this will help him enjoy the training and be eager to perform the entire trick. You can teach the roll over in both directions, using a different command for each way.

"DOWN!"

1 Ask your dog to lie down (see page 15). Sitting on the floor, hold a treat in front of his nose, moving the treat to one side. Encourage your dog to follow your hand.

2 Still holding the treat, move your hand in a circular motion to encourage your dog onto his side. Offer a treat for this position.

"GOOD BOY!"

3 Then, using another treat and more praise and encouragement, get your dog to start to "roll over." Your dog should continue to roll onto his back with all his legs aloft—at this stage it can be a good idea to offer a reward to build confidence.

"ROLL OVER!"

See also...

Get down on it, p. 15

4 When your dog completes the "roll over," provide another treat and plenty of fuss. Repeat these steps until you are only rewarding for the complete "roll over." When your dog is reliably doing this trick, try it using the verbal command "roll over," or the circling hand signal as the command and offer a treat only when finished.

JUMP ON OVER

by SAM

In this trick, your dog will learn to jump over your knee on command. After learning the "jump" (see page 24), your dog can also learn to jump over other obstacles. You will see people asking their dog to jump over a leg while in a standing position. If you want to do this, follow the steps below, then continue training by practicing while sitting in a chair, and then gradually moving into a standing position. The "jump over knee" trick can also be used in heelwork to music (a fun sport that involves the handler and dog performing a routine of heelwork and tricks).

1 Sit on the floor with your legs stretched out. Hold a treat in your hand and move it over your leg, encouraging your dog to follow it by stepping over your leg—at this point, give your dog the treat.

See also...

Jump on a chair, p. 46
Jump through hoops, p. 70

"GOOD BOY!"

2 Repeat step one until your dog is confidently stepping over your legs. As your dog becomes more eager, he will soon start to jump over your legs rather than just step over them. As soon as your dog jumps over, provide a treat and plenty of praise.

"JUMP!"

3 Follow the same steps but this time raise your knees slightly off the floor. When your dog is confidently jumping over your knees, add the command "jump," and reduce the use of the treat so that your dog will respond to only the voice command.

Safety This trick can be very hard on dogs with joint problems, or those with long backs. For a gentler version, only train your dog to step over your outstretched legs.

4 If your dog can jump higher, you could even sit on a chair and do the same steps as above, with your legs outstretched and your feet off the floor. When you start this, you may need to use the treat in your hand again to give your dog the confidence to jump higher.

27

GET YOUR LEASH

by BLITZ

This is an extension to the "fetch" command, and it is important that your dog is confident in fetching toys before you try this trick. Your dog will probably be excited because the leash usually means going out for a fun walk. If you train him to fetch his leash from a specific place on command, your dog will have something useful to do while you look desperately for your keys. For safety, it is a good idea to tie the leash in a knot during training. This way you can prevent your dog's legs from getting tangled up in the leash as it is carried back to you.

"FETCH!"

"GET YOUR LEASH!"

1 Start by playing a game of "fetch" with a favorite toy. Then replace the toy with your dog's leash, throwing it in the same way and rewarding any interest with a treat and some praise.

2 Once your dog is happy to pick up the leash, use the "fetch" command, as before with the toy, to encourage a return.

See also...

Drop it, leave it, p. 17
Go fetch!, p. 19

"DROP IT!"

Top Tip By keeping the leash in the same place and repeating step four, your dog will learn where the leash is kept and will be able to fetch it wherever he is.

3 When your dog is confidently bringing the leash to you, start adding the command "get your leash." By this stage, you should have taught your dog to drop an object on command. When your dog brings the leash to you, put your hand under his chin and say "drop it." This will teach your dog to put the leash in your hand.

"GET YOUR LEASH!"

Top Tip If your dog is not confident in this trick, return to "fetch" training; reward any interest in the leash and progress from there. Once your dog learns this trick, don't be surprised if he interrupts you by dropping his leash in front of you—this is far better than barking or scratching the carpet, so reward his behavior.

4 Now you can train your dog to get the leash from a specific place. Show him where you are putting the leash and gently lead your dog away from the area. Then ask your dog to "get your leash," giving encouragement and the "fetch" command. Give plenty of praise and a treat when your dog brings it to you. Bear in mind that the reward in this trick is the walk as much as the treat!

TRICKS WITH SKILL

SIT PRETTY AND BEG
by JD

This trick may be a challenge, but rewarding your dog for every movement toward the final position will improve confidence and offer plenty of fun along the way. While training, make sure you don't reward your dog at the dinner table—it may look cute but you can end up with a dog that begs for food all day! If you have a long-backed dog, such as a dachshund, you might want to pick another trick, because it can put pressure on your dog's back and he may find it hard to balance.

1 Ask your dog to "sit" (see page 13). Using a treat, get your dog to focus attention on you. This way your dog will know that you are about to do some training.

2 Using the treat, lure your dog into position with an upward hand movement. The front legs should start to lift while your dog's rear stays on the floor. If your dog gets up, say "sit" and start again.

3 Once your dog is balanced, provide a treat. When your dog is reliably staying in position, add the "beg" command or keep using the hand movement. Giving treats intermittently will encourage your dog to hold the "beg" position for longer.

"SIT!"

"BEG!"

Top Tip It may take a long while for your dog to learn to balance in this position, so be patient. If your dog is finding it difficult, keep rewarding the mini steps he takes toward the final position.

FETCH A SPECIFIC ITEM

by RIVA

For this trick, you must first make sure that your dog understands the "fetch" command, and it is also useful if you have taught "get your leash." Now you can progress to training your dog to fetch particular items, depending on the word you are using. Some dog breeds will find this trick easier, especially those bred specifically to retrieve. Find out what motivates your dog and you will be halfway to success. You can even train your dog to fetch more items by name, gradually putting them together in a line. Now that truly is an impressive trick!

"GET THE BALL!"

1 Start by training your dog to fetch an item. Follow the same steps as the "get your leash" trick, replacing the leash with a different item and changing the command to the name of that item. You can train this trick with any item, but a ball is used here.

2 Place the ball in a line of three items approximately 30 feet away from you. For these, use safe objects that your dog would not normally show interest in at first. We want your dog to make the right choice, so don't make it too difficult!

32

Top Tip You can also train your dog to fetch a toy and drop it in your hand so you don't have to bend to pick it up. Place your hand under the toy your dog brings back to you. Say "drop it" when ready to catch it in your hand.

"FETCH THE BALL!"

4 Once your dog is reliably fetching the ball to name, try adding more items, perhaps even other toys that your dog will find exciting. This raises the stakes, so make sure you give plenty of praise as soon as your dog heads for the correct item—and proves how clever he truly is.

See also...

Go fetch!, p. 19
Get your leash, p. 28
Achoo!, p. 66

3 Sit your dog away from the items and ask him to "fetch the ball." Your dog should go to the line of items and pick out the ball. If he does, offer loads of praise and encourage your dog to come back to you with the ball. If your dog picks up the wrong item at this stage, go back to training with the ball on its own and then start adding one extra item at a time to the line.

I SIMPLY REFUSE

by KAI

You may ask, how can this be possible? It truly is, and it is useful if your dog likes to pick up food off the floor or hang around for tasty morsels at mealtimes. This trick can also help to keep your dog safe—with the simple command "leave it," you can prevent your dog from scavenging and swallowing something that could be harmful. Your dog should start to grasp that by leaving the treat in one hand he is rewarded with a treat from your other hand. Eventually, you can leave the first treat in an open hand and your dog will learn not to touch it.

1 Kneel down next to your dog and put a treat in one hand, holding it out flat. Your dog will be able to see the treat, but don't let him take it at this point.

2 As your dog comes toward the treat, close your hand. Your dog will probably sniff at your hand at this point, but just keep your hand closed.

Top Tip Train this trick with food on the floor. Instead of closing your hand with the treat in, begin by picking the food up off the floor so your dog is unable to get it. Your dog will leave food and other items on command, but make sure you have a nice treat to offer in return!

"LEAVE IT!"

"GOOD BOY!"

4 Once your dog has backed away, give praise and a treat from your other hand. When your dog is reliably doing this, add the command "leave it" as you close your hand. Eventually, you can leave the first treat in an open hand and your dog will not touch it.

3 Keep your hand closed as your dog sniffs at the treat. This part may take a while—you have just tempted your dog with something tasty, after all—and be sure to watch your fingers. Be patient and wait until your dog backs away from the food. Remember to lavish him with praise.

See also...

Drop it, leave it, p. 17

HIGH FIVES

by WHISPER

This is an extension of the "shake hands" trick—here, you will train your dog to lift a paw higher, for the "high five" position, which will amaze everyone with how clever he is. First make sure that he is confident performing "shake hands." This trick uses the voice command "high five," but you can use a hand signal instead. You can also try teaching your dog to "high five" your left and right hands with different paws. Dogs with short legs or long backs and larger breeds may find this difficult, so don't ask more of your dog than he can physically handle.

1 Ask your dog to sit and practice the "shake hands" command, giving a reward for the correct position. Once your dog is confident and happy shaking hands, you can progress to the next step.

2 Now move your hand higher and into a more vertical position. As your dog attempts to touch your hand with a paw, give a treat and loads of praise. Each time, move your hand slightly higher and offer treats for any attempts at the "high five."

See also...

Let's shake on it, p. 20

"SHAKE HANDS!"

"HIGH FIVE!"

"GOOD BOY!"

Safety This trick is not suitable for very young or older and arthritic dogs; it can strain their backs.

3 When your dog is touching your hand in the correct position, add the "high five" command and offer a treat with plenty of praise. By repeating the steps with your other hand, using a different command, he will learn to "high five" both hands alternately.

ALL IN A SPIN

by **LEO**

This simple trick teaches your dog to "spin" around in a circle, and is often used as part of a routine where both handler and dog do a set of tricks and heelwork to music. When training the "spin," food is often used to lure a dog around in a circle. However, your dog may prefer a toy. You can get your dog to follow a favorite toy around in a circle to be rewarded with a fun game once the trick is complete. Each time your dog earns a game for the "spin," it will complete the trick faster in anticipation of the toy (and hopefully not get too dizzy!).

1 Stand with your dog in front of you, using a treat to attract attention. Encourage your dog to follow the treat, moving your hand around in a circle above his head.

2 As your dog follows the treat, he should begin to turn, and at this point you may want to provide a reward. As your dog continues to turn, use an encouraging voice. It may be that your dog completes the spin in one attempt. If so, reward your dog with loads of fuss and a treat.

3 When your dog is reliably following your hand movement (moving around in a circle above the dog's head), add the "spin" command. If you would like to teach your dog directional commands, use either "left" or "right" commands. Make sure you are thinking of the directions from your dog's perspective or it can get confusing! Train the other direction by following the same steps above.

"GOOD BOY!"

"SPIN!"

See also...

Sitting pretty, p. 13

BYE-BYE!

by PIPPA

This is a fun trick to use when you would like your dog to say good-bye to family and friends! It is similar to the "high fives" trick, where you train your dog to lift a paw and touch your hand. With patience, this can become a "wave good-bye," but it is best to master "high fives" first. You could progress this trick by teaching your dog to wave with a different paw, using the same steps below but encouraging the other paw by using your other hand. This way your dog will appear to copy you as you wave with alternate hands. Who's clever now?

"HIGH FIVES!"

1 Ask your dog to sit. Practice the "high fives" trick using only the hand signal, where your hand is held high in a vertical position. Give your dog a treat when he touches your hand with a paw.

2 Slightly start to move your hand away from the paw so it is just out of reach from where your dog is sitting. Give your dog a treat every time he raises his paw, even if he doesn't touch your hand.

3 Continue to move your hand away, each time giving your dog a treat and plenty of praise for raising a paw upward, rather than toward you. It is easier for your dog to remain in the sit position with the raised paw. Start adding a waving motion to your hand with each paw raise.

Top Tip It is easier if your dog remains in the sit position while training for this trick, because it will be more difficult to "wave" while standing.

"GOOD GIRL!"

"WAVE PAW!"

4 When your dog is reliably doing the trick in a stationary position, add the command "wave paw" or "say good-bye." If your dog is confident and eager, you can try following the previous steps, using both your hands to encourage your dog to raise both paws for a very enthusiastic wave!

See also...

Sitting pretty, p. 13
Let's shake on it, p. 20
High fives, p. 36

TRICKS WITH FINESSE

DOGGY DANCE

by ALICE

This is a cute trick for your dog to learn and always impresses a crowd! If you would like to train your dog for heelwork to music, this is a favorite to put into any routine. Your dog will stand on his back legs and move around and, if you like a boogie yourself, feel free to join in! This trick is not suitable for breeds with long backs, or those with joint problems, because your dog will need to stand on hind legs and balance for a period of time. If your dog jumps up for attention, be careful when training—this trick can encourage such behavior.

"UP!"

"GOODGIRL!"

"DANCE!"

1 Hold a treat above your dog's head, which will encourage him to stand on hind legs. If your dog has learnt the "jump for joy" trick, he may jump right up in the air, so you will need to give a treat and some fuss as soon as he has lifted his front legs off the floor. Once he is doing so reliably, add the command "up."

2 When your dog is reliably standing on hind legs, you can start to move the treat around. Your dog should follow the treat, effectively "dancing" on hind legs. Remember to give your dog plenty of praise.

3 Once your dog is following the treat and staying in the standing position, you can add the command "dance." Start to reduce the use of the treat in your hand until your dog is responding to either "dance" or the signal of your hand above your dog's head, with fingers wiggling.

See also...

Jump for joy, p. 24

41

CARRY MY PURSE

by FERN

Similar to the tricks "get your leash" or "fetch a specific item," this trick takes things up a notch, training your dog to walk alongside you with the purse in his mouth using the verbal command "carry." This is handy when you have to carry shopping bags. Be careful not to completely trust your dog with a valued item—he may wander off with it when your back is turned. Or, if your dog is young and likes to chew, you may want to avoid training tricks that encourage an interest in expensive items. Best to use an old purse with no money in it!

"FETCH THE PURSE!"

1 First you must train your dog to fetch your purse by name, as shown in the "get your leash" trick, replacing the leash with the purse. Be patient, because this can take time to master.

2 When your dog fetches your purse, start to delay offering a treat until your purse is carried for a little longer. Do this by walking away as your dog brings the purse toward you. Provide plenty of praise for continuing to hold the purse as you move away.

"GOOD GIRL!"

4 Once your dog has mastered the art of carrying your purse, start adding the command "carry." Offer a treat from the purse after you"ve taken it back. Your dog will be less likely to abandon the purse if there are treats inside. Politely thank your dog for doing such a good deed!

Top Tip If your dog drops the purse, don't pick it up. Simply point to it and ask him to fetch it. Of course, you can train your dog to carry other items, such as toys, while walking. This way, when that beloved ball is all wet and muddy in the park, you don't have to pick it up!

3 Pat your leg to encourage your dog to come to you. Continue walking while your dog walks beside you carrying the purse, providing a treat and taking the purse once it has been carried for a little while. Slowly build up the time your dog holds the purse before handing out each successive treat.

See also...

Get your leash, p. 28
Fetch a specific item, p. 32
Find the keys, p. 56

WALK AND WEAVE

by SAM

This is one of the harder tricks to train, but it can look impressive to your friends! Dogs truly love doing this trick, because it gives both brain and body a good workout, and it's fun on a walk. Your dog will learn to weave in and out of your legs as you are walking—and if you want a challenge, you can even try it while jogging! If this becomes old news, try walking backward. It can all be done, but know which way your dog should be going before starting any training. With a plan in place, you and your dog can work confidently through each step.

"GOOD BOY!"

1 Ask your dog to sit next to your legs on your right. Take a large step forward with your left leg and hold the position. Hold a treat in your right hand and start to move it under your legs, encouraging your dog to follow it.

2 When your dog walks through your legs, swap the treat into your left hand so he can continue to follow it. Give your dog the treat as he comes out the other side. Repeat these steps until your dog is confidently weaving through one leg.

"WEAVE!"

See also...

Agility poles, p. 74

3 As your dog walks through, step forward with your right leg, using a treat to lure him back through the other way. Your dog should do a complete weave through your legs as you walk two steps. Start to delay the first treat, providing a treat only for a complete weave.

4 When your dog is reliably following your hand, start to remove the treat and reduce the movement of your hand, so you are only pointing through your legs. You can also add the command "weave." Add more steps until your dog continues weaving through your legs for the treat at the end.

Top Tip This trick is very popular with border collies who excel at agility. As you can imagine, some dogs are too big to do this trick—unless you have very long legs.

JUMP ON A CHAIR

by KAI

Only use "jump on a chair" as a trick, and always put it in a command to discourage your dog from jumping on furniture. If your dog already does this—or if you harbor deep suspicions that such events happen when you are out—it can be better to turn this misdeed into a learned command. That way you can stop your sofa from getting messy after a muddy walk. You can progress your dog to jump onto other surfaces, which can help when training some of the more advanced tricks. Make sure these surfaces are safe, not slippery, and not too high.

"GOOD BOY!"

1 Find a safe—and preferably inexpensive—chair your dog can comfortably sit on. Ask your dog to sit in front of the chair while you stand on the other side of it. With treat in hand, encourage your dog to put his front feet onto the chair by patting the chair.

2 When your dog puts his front feet onto the chair, offer the treat in your hand and plenty of praise. If your dog is unsure, you may need to just give a reward for putting one foot onto the chair and break the training into smaller steps.

46

"JUMP ON!"

3 With another treat in your hand, encourage your dog to jump right onto the chair. When sitting nicely in the chair—but not getting too comfortable—provide a treat. Once your dog is reliably jumping onto the chair, add the command "jump on" just as he gets onto the chair.

Safety This trick is not ideal for large, long-backed, or older dogs.

"OFF!"

Top tip If your dog is reluctant to jump on the chair, don't worry—try the trick in stages. If in doubt, find another trick that your dog seems to enjoy.

See also...

Jump through hoops, p. 70
Stay put on a table, p. 78

4 Now the harder part. Lure your dog off the chair with a treat, so he learns to jump off calmly. When he is doing so reliably, you can add the command "off." You can practice this trick on different chairs but make sure you and your dog are always safe—don't use one with wheels or that may move when your dog jumps on and off.

IN YOUR BED

by FERN

This is a simple trick that can be used in many different situations. It will help encourage your dog to settle while you are eating dinner. The trick can also help prevent your dog from jumping up, and by simply having the bed near the front door you can even encourage your dog to settle as visitors come in. Building up the training slowly will help your dog to settle even around the most tempting distractions. Never be stern when asking your dog to go to bed, so he sees it as a good place to go instead of a place to be sent to for bad behavior.

"DOWN!"

1 First, practice the "down" command with your dog. Release your dog from the down position, then place a treat in the bed to get your dog's attention.

2 Your dog will probably take a step into his bed and try to eat the food. Remember to praise your dog for any effort toward the "in your bed" position.

"GOOD GIRL!"

48

"DOWN!"

3 Using another treat, lure your dog fully onto the bed, offering encouragement to lie down. As your dog lies down, give the treat and some praise.

"IN YOUR BED!"

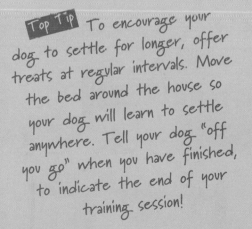

Top Tip To encourage your dog to settle for longer, offer treats at regular intervals. Move the bed around the house so your dog will learn to settle anywhere. Tell your dog "off you go" when you have finished, to indicate the end of your training session!

See also...

Get down on it, p. 15

4 Repeat the steps above and, as your dog begins to lie down, add the command "in your bed" and provide a reward. When your dog is reliably responding to the command, reduce the use of the treat in your hand. This way your dog will start to learn to go to the bed on command and you will be able to ask from farther away. You can use a hand signal at this stage instead, such as a pointing finger.

Tricks with finesse

CLEAN AND TIDY

by KAI

Have you ever entered the living room to find your dog has emptied the toy box all over the floor? Well, now you can train your dog to tidy up after a playing session. In this trick, your dog will learn to pick up one toy at a time from the floor and place it gently into a toy box. First, teach your dog the "drop it, leave it" trick and the "fetch a specific item" trick. Put the two together and you have yourself one tidy dog! If you lose something, it may be worth checking in the toy box—your dog might get carried away and "tidy" your belongings, too!

"FETCH THE TOY!"

1 Find a suitable toy box—not too small—and a favorite toy. With your dog's attention, place the box in front of him and stand yourself behind it. Show your dog the toy and place it on the floor next to the box. Ask your dog to "fetch the toy."

"DROP IT!"

2 Your dog should try to bring it to you, so make sure you stand so that the box is between you and your dog. When his head is above the toy box with the toy in his mouth, point into the box and ask your dog to "drop it."

50

3 If you get your timing right, your dog will drop it into the box. Provide a treat with plenty of praise when the toy lands in the box. Repeat this until your dog is reliably dropping the toy into the box. Now say "clean up" when your dog goes to pick up the toy.

"CLEAN UP!"

Top Tip To progress with this trick you will need to move the box away from you gradually. It can be harder for your dog to put his toys away in the box when he is farther away from you. Make sure you don't move on too quickly—this trick takes time to perfect.

4 Gradually start to move the box away from you, repeating the above steps. Don't move on too quickly—this trick takes patience. Start to introduce other toys onto the floor, so that your dog learns to "clean up" all the toys in the room one by one. Remember the all-important treat for each toy dropped in the box. When he has mastered this, give him a treat only when every second or third toy is put in the basket.

See also...

Drop it, leave it, p. 17
Fetch a specific item, p. 32

BALANCE AND CATCH

by PECAN

This trick teaches your dog to balance a treat on his nose and, at your command, throw it in the air and then catch it. Wow! Most dogs will love this trick, although it can be a challenge to train, so be patient. To make it easier for this trick to work, master "the balance" and "the catch" separately, working on each step as an individual exercise. In addition, make sure that you choose a large and flat treat that will easily balance on your dog's nose. Don't rush it. Take things slowly and keep a sense of fun—your dog will!

"STILL!"

1 Using the "sit" command, place your hand under your dog's chin, so that his head rests in your hand. With your other hand, reveal but withhold a treat, moving it gradually over your dog's nose. If your dog's head remains still, provide a treat. To progress, add the command "still" and phase out the use of your hand under the chin.

2 To complete the balance stage, next, place a treat onto your dog's nose. This will be the eventual reward, but when first doing this, have a treat in your other hand to reduce the temptation!

See also...

Sitting pretty, p. 13

"CATCH!"

Top Tip Although it may take some time for your dog to learn to hold its head still, be patient—it's better for your dog to learn without being forced.

3 Now you need to focus your dog on the catch stage. First, practice throwing the treat until your dog can catch it as it falls. Once your dog is reliably catching the treat, use the "catch" command just before it lands in the mouth. Your dog may start to watch your hand movement as you throw the treat—this can be used as a hand signal later on.

4 Now you can combine both commands together. Ask your dog to sit and give the "still" command. With the treat balanced, pretend to throw a treat in the air and say "catch"—your dog should lift his head, flick the treat up, and catch it as it falls. Don't worry if your dog doesn't catch it first time—practice makes perfect!

ACTING SHY

by KAI

This trick is a difficult one and will take time and patience to perfect, so reward your dog for even small steps forward. However, your dog will look particularly cute, so it is well worth the effort! The trick involves a brand new behavior that involves your dog resting his head on the floor. If your dog "acts shy" with one paw initially, start to withhold the treat and wait for the behavior with two paws. When this happens, give your dog plenty of praise, with a treat, to encourage him to repeat the "two paws" behavior.

"WAVE PAW!"

1 Practice the "bye-bye!" trick with your dog, while he is in a sitting position, giving plenty of fuss and treats when it's done correctly. Once perfected, practice waving with both paws, for further treats, of course.

"DOWN!"

2 Now ask your dog to lie down and give the command for a wave. Your dog may find this more difficult from a down position, but give loads of praise and a treat for any small attempt at lifting either paw from the ground.

"GOOD BOY!"

3 With step two mastered, keep your dog in the "down" position. Hold a treat on the floor in front of your dog and encourage him to lower his head to the ground, giving a reward and praise for success. Train your dog to hold the position longer by waiting a few seconds before giving each successive treat.

"SHY!"

Top Tip Remember to keep sessions short and end on a good note. It will take time for your dog to understand what the treat is for, so don't expect to progress too quickly, and work in small steps.

See also...

Sitting pretty, p. 13
Get down on it, p. 15
Bye-bye! p. 38

4 With your dog's head to the ground, move to one side of him, asking for a wave. Your dog will try and wave toward you—as soon as he moves his paw closer to his nose, provide a treat. When your dog is reliably doing this with either paw, add the command "shy," with a much-deserved treat for success.

FIND THE KEYS

by BLITZ

For this trick to be a success, you will first need to train your dog to fetch the keys by, name using the steps used in the "fetch a specific item" trick. Once mastered, "find the keys" means that you will always have a willing helper for those "search the pockets" moments. All for a simple treat or praise in return. Some dogs are unsure about picking up keys due to the feel of metal. Attach a piece of cloth or a toy to the key ring, to make it easier to pick up. Over time, you can reduce the size of the toy until your dog is happy to pick up the keys on his own.

"STAY!"

"FIND THE KEYS!"

1 Train your dog to "fetch" the keys from a selection of items. Now add the "sit" and "stay" commands, letting your dog watch as you put the keys onto the ground a short distance away.

2 Go back to your dog and say "find the keys." Your dog may sniff around in the grass at first, but when the keys are found, give your dog a lot of fuss (especially if you wondered if you'd truly lost them!) and encourage him to come back to you.

See also...

Sitting pretty, p. 13
Staying power, p. 14
Fetch a specific item, p. 32

"GOOD BOY!"

4 Once your dog is reliably finding the keys in easier hiding places, progress to harder ones, or try hiding the keys when your dog isn't looking. Don't forget to give your dog encouragement while working through the steps. As soon as your dog has found the keys, ask him to bring them back and invite him to give them to you.

3 If your dog successfully retrieves the keys and brings them back to you, reward him with a treat and plenty of praise. Now repeat the steps, this time putting the keys in a less obvious place. At this stage, add the "sit" and "stay" commands, so your dog can still watch where you hide them.

Top Tip It will take time before your dog can find the keys when even you don't know where they are. In training, if your dog looks unsure, give plenty of encouragement when closer to the keys and trust him to eventually "sniff" them out.

CLOSE THAT DOOR

by KAI

This can be a very useful trick if you are sitting comfortably indoors and there is a chilly breeze through an open door! Although this seems a difficult trick to train, it is straightforward, but it is best you don't encourage your dog to do this on doors that lock shut. If you have nice new doors that you don't want to be scratched, this may not be the trick for you. Be warned that your dog could try and close doors unasked, and may even try it in other people's houses. Be patient and work through the stages gradually—it will be worth it in the end!

1 Hold a treat high up next to a closed door and encourage your dog to jump up to reach for the treat. When your dog jumps up against the door, actually hitting it, offer the treat with loads of praise.

"GOOD BOY!"

Safety This trick is not suitable for older dogs or those with back problems, because it can put pressure on their joints.

2 Open the door very slightly. Repeat step one, but this time when your dog jumps up at the door, his weight should cause the door to close. Your dog may be a little unsure if the door makes a noise when it shuts. So, encourage him back up on the closed door and reward him while he is the correct position on two paws.

Top tip This trick only works with doors that you can push to close. Training your dog to pull a door shut is more difficult, but can be achieved if you attach a ball on a rope to the door, then train your dog to pull the ball to shut the door.

"GOOD BOY!"

"CLOSE THE DOOR!"

4 When your dog is reliably responding to the "close the door" command, move farther away before asking him to close it. You can open the door wider so your dog has to put a bit more effort in. Don't forget to hand out warm praise and that treat!

3 When your dog is confidently closing the door, start adding the command "close the door" just before he jumps up. You also need to reduce the use of your hand pointing and moving toward the door, so that your dog starts to respond to the command without needing this signal.

OPENING DOORS

You can use a similar method to train your dog to open doors, although you will need to teach him to move the handle as well as jump up at the door. Again, this is harder if the door pulls to open. Keep in mind that once you have trained your dog to open a door, no room in the house is off limits!

CREEPY CRAWLIES

by PIPPA

This is an impressive trick for your dog to learn. At first, your dog will learn to crawl toward you, but given time and practice, he"ll be crawling in any direction, even away from you. If your dog gets up from the down position during training, try using food to lure him under a low barrier, such as an outstretched leg. This will encourage your dog to stay in the down position. If you want to make this trick even more impressive, your dog can learn to crawl while weaving in and out of your legs as you walk!

"DOWN!"

1 Kneel down on the floor and ask your dog to lie down in front of you. Show your dog you have a particularly nice treat in your hand.

2 Hold the treat on the floor between your dog's front legs, and slowly move it away from his nose, just out of reach. If your dog gets up from the down position, remove the treat, ask him to lie down, and try again.

3 When your dog starts moving toward the treat very slightly, offer the treat and plenty of praise. Continue to reward very small movements toward the treat without your dog getting out of the down position, so your dog starts to "crawl" toward the treat.

"GOOD GIRL!"

Top Tip If your dog starts getting up from the down position at any stage, go back a step and reward him for crawling a shorter distance. You could place a treat under your foot to keep his attention downward. Be generous with even small successes.

"CRAWL!"

4 Once your dog is reliably crawling toward the treat, start to add the "crawl" command and reduce the use of the treat in your hand. You can train your dog to crawl farther by delaying giving the treat for a slightly longer crawl.

See also...

Get down on it, p. 15
All in a spin, p. 37
Walk and weave, p. 44

SCENT TRAIL

by ALICE

Dogs naturally use their noses to search for food and toys, so this trick provides loads of interest. It follows the principles used for dogs working on search-and-rescue teams, where the dog learns to follow the scent trails left by people as they walk. With the simple command "seek," you can teach your dog to follow a trail left by food. Start the training in a low-distraction area, such as in the house or yard, with few other scents present. If your dog tends to find a lot of food out on walks, be careful because this training may increase the scavenging!

See also...

Sitting pretty, p. 13
Staying power, p. 14
Get down on it, p. 15

"SIT!" "STAY!"

"SEEK!"

1 Find some tasty treats that your dog will enjoy. Using the "sit/stay" commands, allow your dog to watch you lay the scent trail by dragging one of the treats along the floor in a straight line. Drop treats at various intervals along the trail and at the end place a few in a pile.

2 Encourage your dog to start sniffing the scent trail by pointing to the start of the trail and adding the command "seek." The smell of the treats on the floor should keep your dog moving quickly toward the first treat.

"GOOD GIRL!"

Top Tip Progress your dog's training by making the trail more complicated, with corners, obstacles, and other scents—a big park is perfect. Eventually, you can make it harder by having short "breaks" in the scent trail, so your dog has to search and pick up the trail again. You can progress to hiding treats in another room for an even bigger challenge!

3 When your dog finds the treat, give plenty of praise. Let your dog carry on sniffing, following the trail and eating the treats along the way. If you need to, put more treats along the trail to keep your dog focused.

4 At the end of the trail, your dog should receive a jackpot reward for finishing the trick. When your dog is confident, gradually reduce the number of treats on the trail until your dog simply follows the scent with his nose to the end for the big reward.

GIVE ME POWER!

by KAI

This trick teaches your dog to pull a cord switch to turn on or off an old ceiling light or fan. At first, this trick requires a pull cord that can be moved around. Before trying it on a fixture, make sure it is sturdy and the cord is not wrapped around fan blades. You can also train your dog to use wall switches, but most dogs find them hard to reach. You can start with a light switch not attached to the wall, training your dog to touch it with his paw when it is in your hand. Then move the switch around until your dog understands the command "turn on light/fan."

"GOOD BOY!"

1 Use a light pull or a piece of string with a knot at the end to teach the "pull" before trying it with a real pull switch. Encourage your dog to show interest in the string by moving it around the floor or in the air.

See also...

Let's shake on it, p. 20

2 As soon as your dog starts to take hold of the string with his mouth, tell him "good boy" and offer a treat. Repeat this until your dog is happy and confident to hold the string.

"TURN ON LIGHT/FAN!"

3 While your dog is holding the string, start to gently pull it away. As your dog becomes frustrated, he should start to tug the other way. When he does, give plenty of praise and a treat. When your dog is reliably pulling at the string, start adding the "turn on light/fan" command.

4 Transfer your dog to the real pull switch. This may be harder if it is high up (you can extend it), but encourage your dog and ask him to "pull." Reward your dog at first for just pulling at the string—over time, give a treat and loads of praise for switching the light or fan on or off.

"GOOD BOY!"

Safety This trick is not suitable for young puppies, older dogs, those with joint problems, or a giant breed, because it puts pressure on the joints when the dog jumps up and down.

65

Tricks with finesse

ACHOO!

by SAM

Your dog will need to know how to "fetch" before starting this trick. Instead of learning to fetch the tissue by name, your dog will learn to fetch a tissue when you "sneeze." The "sneeze" becomes the command to ask your dog to fetch the tissue. Start with the box of tissues on the floor and gradually progress to having it on higher surfaces, such as a table, where you would normally keep them. If your dog likes to chew, you may find he prefers to chew up the tissue rather than bringing it back! In this case, try a handkerchief.

"FETCH A TISSUE!"

1 First encourage your dog to show interest in a box of tissues. Move the box around and eventually he should start to take hold of the tissues that are sticking out. At this point, give your dog a treat.

2 Ask your dog to fetch a tissue and encourage him back to you as you have done previously with the "fetch" command. Continue practicing "fetch" with one of the tissues, and keep replacing the tissue back in the box.

66

"ACHOO!"

3 When your dog is confidently bringing the tissue to you, add the "sneeze" (by making an "achoo" sound while placing your hands over your nose) just as he is about to pick up a tissue from the box. As your dog continues to pick up the tissue, tell him that he is a good boy and provide a tasty treat.

Top Tip In time, your dog will learn to go to find the box of tissues when you sneeze, but this will be easier if you always keep them in the same place.

"GOOD BOY!"

4 Your dog will soon learn that when you sneeze, he gets a reward and praise for picking up the tissue and bringing it to you. Over time and with more practice, your dog will need less help and you won't need to show the tissue before you sneeze.

See also...

Go fetch! p. 19
Fetch a specific item, p. 32

67

FEATS OF AGILITY

THROUGH THE TUNNEL

by HULA

This is a popular agility exercise that most dogs love. For training practice, you can use an open tunnel designed for children, as long as your dog is not too big. Some dogs can be a little unsure at first, so when starting out, make sure your dog can see all the way through and that the tunnel is held steady. If you progress to working quickly, use safe agility equipment that will remain stable when your dog runs through. Once your dog has built up confidence, he might be able to go through a curved tunnel without being able to see the end.

1 As you approach the tunnel, let your dog see you throw a toy inside. Make eye contact with your dog and coax him toward you. Your dog should enter the tunnel to get it and come straight out again. At this point, don't expect your dog to go all the way through. First let your dog gain confidence going inside.

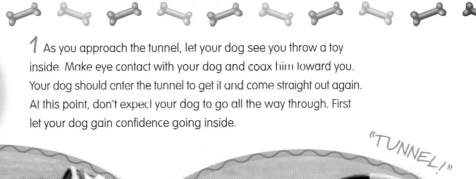

"TUNNEL!"

2 Once your dog is happy going inside, throw the toy farther into the tunnel. While your dog is inside, run along with him to the other end to encourage him to reach the end of the tunnel, providing a game with the toy, or a treat when he exits. When your dog is reliably going in, just pretend to throw the toy. As your dog runs in to find it, call him through, giving him the toy at the other end.

3 Once your dog is confident with steps one and two, add the command "tunnel" and continue the action of throwing a toy. This hand movement can eventually become the hand signal. You can then progress to a curved tunnel, so your dog runs around a corner inside.

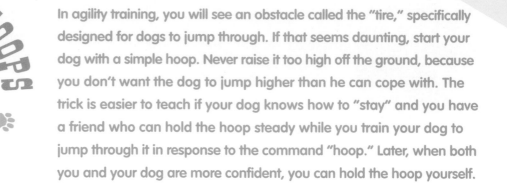

JUMP THROUGH HOOPS
by CEDAR

In agility training, you will see an obstacle called the "tire," specifically designed for dogs to jump through. If that seems daunting, start your dog with a simple hoop. Never raise it too high off the ground, because you don't want the dog to jump higher than he can cope with. The trick is easier to teach if your dog knows how to "stay" and you have a friend who can hold the hoop steady while you train your dog to jump through it in response to the command "hoop." Later, when both you and your dog are more confident, you can hold the hoop yourself.

"SIT!"

1 Ask your friend to hold the hoop low to the ground. Ask your dog to "sit" on one side of the hoop. Walk around to the other side so that you are facing your dog. Hold a treat out in your hand so that it's in your dog's line of vision, but far enough for your dog to have to walk forward to reach it.

"COME!"

2 Encourage your dog to follow the treat and step through the hoop, using the command "come." As soon as he does, give your dog the treat and plenty of praise. Repeat this until he is confidently stepping through. If your dog prefers toys, you can use a toy to lure him through the hoop.

Safety This trick is not suitable for dogs with joint problems because it involves jumping. Never ask a dog to jump higher than the level of his shoulder—you run the risk of placing too much strain on his joints and muscles. You can keep the hoop low by the ground for older dogs, so they can just step through it and still enjoy learning a new trick!

3 Gradually raise the hoop higher, so your dog begins to jump through it. If using a toy, throw it through for him to follow. Start to add the command "hoop" as your dog is about to jump through. Don't forget to always give your dog a treat or toy at the end!

"HOOP!"

4 If you want to take this trick further, try the tire. In agility training, you will want your dog to jump through the tire while you run beside him. You can work on this by moving to the side of the tire when you call your dog through.

Top Tip Over time, you want to reduce the use of any treats or toys in your hand. In agility competitions, you cannot take treats or toys into the ring, so your dog needs to learn to jump through the tire on command with no lure.

See also...

Sitting pretty, p. 13
Staying power, p. 14
Jump on over, p. 26
Hurdle jumping, p. 76

TOUCH AND GO

by KIA

There are three obstacles in agility: the seesaw, the dog walk, and the A frame, where your dog has to walk up and over, touching the start and end of the obstacle without jumping over a marker at the bottom. This marker is called a "contact" and is a different color so it stands out. Use a touch target that is flat and transparent, because it is easier to practice with when it is placed over a contact. By training your dog to touch a contact, you can achieve high standards on the agility circuit and maybe even win yourself—and your dog—a couple of rosettes!

1 Find yourself an item, such as a plastic lid, to use as your touch target. Place this on the floor in front of your dog. Hopefully your dog will show enough interest in the target to sniff it with his nose. As he does this, give him loads of praise and provide a treat.

Top Tip If your dog does not show any interest in the target, try placing a treat on it. When your dog shows interest in food on the target, reward him for touching it.

"GOOD GIRL!"

"TOUCH!"

2 Repeat this exercise with your dog, rewarding your dog each time he touches the target. When your dog is reliably touching the target, add the command "touch." You can then start moving the target around, using the "touch" command to send your dog to touch the target wherever it may be.

3 Start with a plank of wood, keeping it flat for safety. Teach your dog to run along the plank, guiding him with a treat. When your dog is happy doing this, introduce the touch target at the end of the plank, or dog walk if you are using one at this point (as shown here), teaching him to stop on the "contact" before he runs off.

Top Tip If you want to progress with agility with your dog to a high level, it is better to attend a class where an agility instructor can help you work with all the equipment safely.

4 Once your dog is confident stopping on the contact with the touch target, you can remove the target, remembering to give a reward for stopping in the right place. It is important in agility that your dog touches two contacts at both ends of each obstacle. It is easier for your dog to touch the contact at the start on the way up, but he is more likely to jump over the contact at the end on the way down.

"GOOD GIRL!"

AGILITY POLES

by PIPPA

It is well known that border collies are famous for doing agility tricks, but with enough patience any breed can do this highly enjoyable trick. You can first teach your dog the "walk and weave" trick, so he learns the movement required. You can get professional weave poles or simply use some plastic poles, along with spacers to set them 20–22 inches apart. This is one of the hardest tricks in the book to get right, so try not to rush your training, and never forget to offer your dog plenty of praise and treats for tackling such a difficult trick.

"GOOD GIRL!"

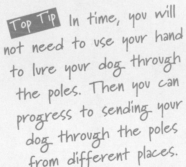

Top Tip In time, you will not need to use your hand to lure your dog through the poles. Then you can progress to sending your dog through the poles from different places.

1 Show your dog the treat in your hand, and stand him next to the poles, on your **left**. Your dog should enter from the **right** of the poles so that he turns **left** first. Move your hand away from you and between the first two poles. Once your dog follows, offer the treat and some praise.

2 With another treat in your hand, lure your dog back toward you between the second and third poles, offering it when your dog goes through the poles. Repeat this until your dog has "weaved" all his way through, and give plenty of fuss and praise for a job well done.

3 Repeat the previous steps until you see your dog start to predict which way to go. When this improves, start to only give your dog a treat when he has weaved through two poles. Progress to three, and then give your dog a treat only at the end of the six poles, as well as plenty of praise for a job well done.

"WEAVE!"

4 When your dog is confident, add the command word "weave" when he enters the poles and as he continues through them. Your dog should speed up with practice, but it will take time. Don't rush it, and if your dog ever misses a pole, return to steps one and two and reward at every turn.

See also...

Walk and weave, p. 44

HURDLE JUMPING

by HULA

When you start training this trick, keep the jump low enough for your dog to first gain confidence—it takes a lot of self belief to become a high jump star. If you plan to compete in agility, it pays to teach your dog to turn left or right on command—work on the "all in a spin" trick until your dog is confident to turn left or right, wherever you are. Try running along next to your dog while teaching the left and right commands. When you progress this to jumping, you will need an added incentive—your dog's favorite toy should "do the trick."

"JUMP!"

"RIGHT!"

1 First follow the same steps that are used in the "jump through hoops" trick, using a low jump. Once your dog is confident, add the "jump" command. Make sure your dog is happy to jump when you are running beside him before you move on to directed jumping.

2 Set up a low jump and practice right turns. With the dog on your left, run toward the jump, using the "jump" command. As your dog jumps, say "right" and turn right, away from the jump. As your dog turns toward you, throw his toy to the right, giving plenty of praise and a game with the toy.

Safety Jumping may not
be suitable for some dogs
with joint problems or
certain giant breeds. The
size of your dog will also
determine the size of
the jumps required
for competitions.

3 Repeat step two with your dog on your right—that is, with your dog turning away from you. Make sure you throw the toy to your dog's right and provide a game with the toy for a successful turn.

4 Add a second jump, at a right angle to your first jump, and send your dog over it using directional commands. Eventually, you can start using more jumps and guide your dog around a short course. Do the same steps with the left turn, practicing with your dog on both sides of you.

See also...

All in a spin, p. 37
Jump through hoops, p. 70

STAY PUT ON A TABLE

by KIA

This trick can be part of an agility course and involves your dog jumping onto a table, lying down, and waiting before moving on to the next obstacle. Your dog should know the commands "down" and "stay" before tackling it. Even if you are not entering a competition, it is a useful trick because it encourages obedience. Your dog will need to stay for five seconds in competitions, but you can practice a longer amount. A low, nonslip table is appropriate to start with. Most agility clubs have different-size tables with nonslip surfaces that are ideal.

"GOOD GIRL!"

"DOWN!"

2 When your dog is on the table, give him the command "down" and provide a reward. Once your dog is happy jumping on the table and lying down, practice a short stay by gradually moving away and then coming back, offering a treat for remaining in the down position.

1 Find a safe low table and encourage your dog to put his front feet onto it, offering a treat and praise. If your dog is confidently doing this, you can ask a little more of him. Place a treat in the middle of the table, and encourage him to jump right onto it with the command "jump on." His reward is the treat and even more fuss.

"OFF!"

3 When your dog has remained on the table for a few seconds, call him down with the command "off" and practice again. Repeat the steps until your dog starts to lie down automatically once on the table. At this point, start introducing a command, such as "table."

INDEX

Dog Gallery

Thank you!

Parragon would like to say a big thank you to Nick Ridley and staff at the Hearing Dogs for Deaf People (www.hearingdogs.org.uk), who offered their help at the photo shoots. Special mention goes to all the dogs, who couldn't have performed better or been more delightful to work with.

ABI · ALICE · BLITZ · CEDAR · FERN

HULA · JD · KAI · KIA · LEO

PECAN · PIPPA · RIVA · SAM · WHISPER